1 Draw around your picture onto a piece of card. Cut out the centre 0.5cm smaller than your picture and the outer edge 5cm larger.

2 Cut or break the twigs into short lengths and glue all around the sides of the card.

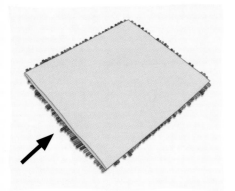

3 Cut a piece of card the same size as the frame, glue along three edges and stick to the back of the frame. The unglued edge is so you can slide in your picture.

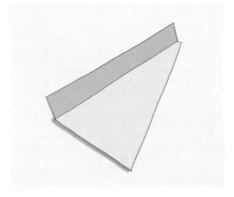

4 Cut out a triangular piece of card to act as a strut and cut off its top, then fold a line 2cm along its edge.

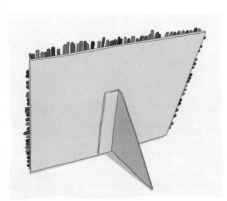

5 Glue the strut to the back of the frame. Add your picture!

2 TWIGGY PICTURE FRAME

Use your next walk in the countryside or park to look for twigs for this textured picture frame. Try to collect lots of different colours and don't pick up any with thorns!

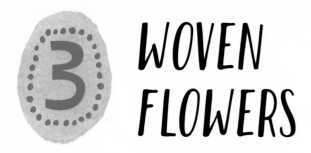

3 WOVEN FLOWERS

Weave a bunch of flowers for a great gift or just to brighten up your room. Attach a safety pin to the back and turn them into pretty brooches, too.

1 Draw around the flower template on coloured card and cut out. Use a pencil to pierce a hole in the centre, then feed a length of wool through the hole.

2 Tie the loose end around the flower with a knot. This forms the first loop. Then thread the wool between each petal and the centre hole.

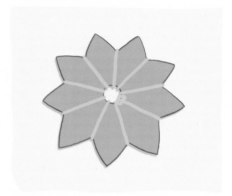

3 Continue until the wool forms an outline for all the petals. Then tie off at the back.

4 On the flower's front, tie on more wool to one of the petal strands and start to weave to create the centre. Go under, then over the petal strands repeatedly.

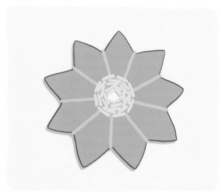

5 When you have made a big enough centre, tie a knot and tuck the end under the weaving.

6 Use a variety of coloured card to make different flower designs. Use the template provided for leaves. Add straws to the back to create stems.

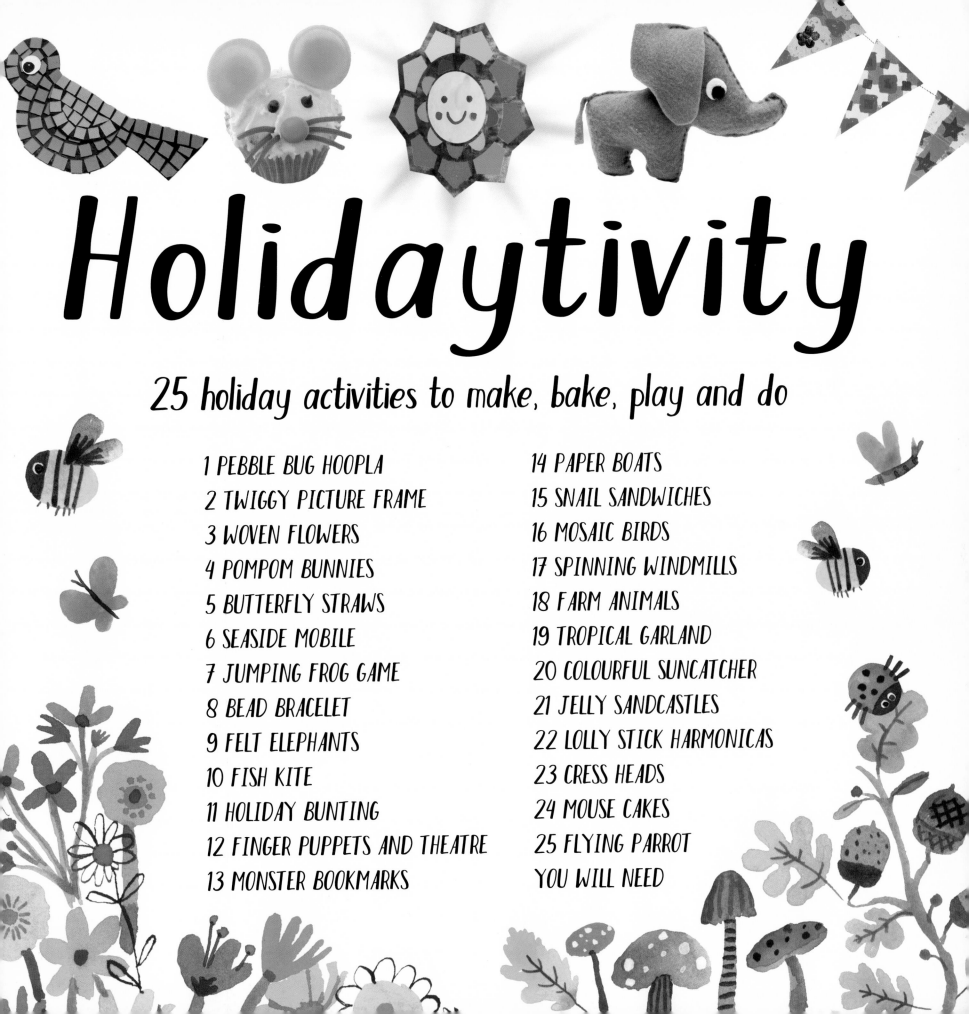

Holidaytivity

25 holiday activities to make, bake, play and do

PEBBLE BUG HOOPLA

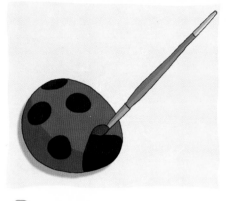

Use pebbles to make the targets for this fun game. Paint them to look like real insects or invent your own wacky bugs!

1 Decide the type of bug you want to create and use bright colours to paint the bug patterns on your pebble.

2 Cut narrow strips of black felt for the legs and glue to the base of the bug. How many legs does your bug have?

3 Once you've made a selection of bugs, press out the eyes and wings from the card sheet and glue them to your bugs.

4 Cut out rings from coloured card with holes just big enough to fit over your bugs.

5 Lay your bugs on the floor, then take a few steps back and throw the rings, aiming to trap your pebble bugs inside them.

POMPOM BUNNIES

These fluffy bunnies are a perfect Easter holiday gift. So re-use your pompom makers to create a whole family. The more the merrier!

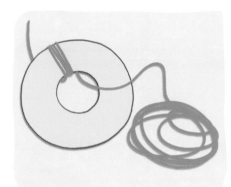

1 Take the pompom makers from the card sheets. Put together large (body), medium (head) and small (tail) rings and begin wrapping wool around them.

2 Keep wrapping the wool around the rings until there's only a very small hole left in the middle.

3 Cut around the edge of the woollen ring. You may have to snip a few layers at a time until you reach the cardboard rings.

4 Carefully pull the cardboard rings slightly apart to create a groove. Tie a length of wool tightly around the middle, then remove the cardboard rings completely.

5 Once you've repeated steps 1–4 to create all three body parts, use the template to cut a pair of ears from felt. Pinch their bases together and glue to hold.

6 Glue the head and tail pompoms to the body, then the ears. Finally, press out the eyes and nose from the card sheet and glue them to the head.

5 BUTTERFLY STRAWS

Serve your drinks with these fluttering butterfly straws and cups and set the tone for a memorable, fun-packed holiday!

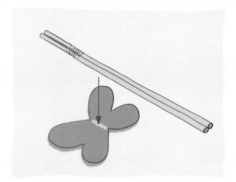

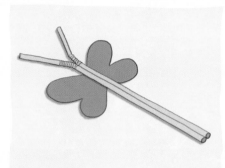

1 Press out one of the card butterflies. Tape two bendy straws together and glue to the back of the butterfly.

2 Bend the tops of the straws outwards so they look like the butterfly's antennae.

3 Draw around the butterfly templates on different coloured paper to make a variety of butterflies.

4 Glue the paper butterflies onto the paper cups and use coloured pencils to add more detail and other patterns.

6 SEASIDE MOBILE

Missing the beach already? Hang this beach-inspired mobile in your room and you will be dreaming of the beach all year long.

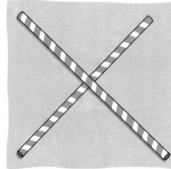

1 Press out the illustrated pieces at the back of the book.

2 Glue two paper straws together for your mobile frame.

3 Make a small hole at the top of each of the mobile pieces and thread through some string.

4 Tie to the straws at different lengths. Hang up and watch the sea creatures swim around.

1 Press out the frog. Follow the dotted lines on the unprinted side to fold one corner, open it up and repeat fold to other corner to create a cross shape of folds.

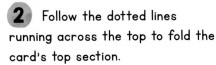

2 Follow the dotted lines running across the top to fold the card's top section.

Who will win the great jumping frog game? Make these four frogs race each other around the pond and see who can land on the lily flowers first.

3 Fold the corners in carefully so that you are left with a triangle shape at the top.

4 Fold back the two bottom corners of the triangle. Then fold in the long edges at either side.

5 Turn the card over and fold into a Z shape along the dotted lines to make your frog stand up. Flick your fingers over his back and watch him jump! Repeat steps 1-5 to make the other frogs.

6 Draw around the other templates onto card to make the lily pads and double-layered flowers. Cut out and glue these to a large piece of blue card to make the pond.

8 BEAD BRACELET

Make original gifts for your friends with this funky bead jewellery, made out of coloured paper!

1 Trace around one of the bead templates at the back of this book onto coloured paper and cut out. Roll around a pencil from the thick end.

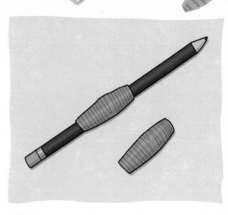

2 Glue the end and slide off: your first bead! Make up more bead (approx. 15) using different coloure paper. Use one template (pictured) or a variety from those provided.

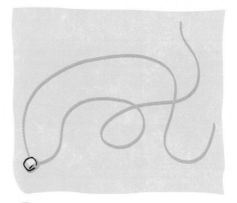

3 Cut a 150cm piece of thin elastic and tie a plastic bead in its middle to act as a fastener.

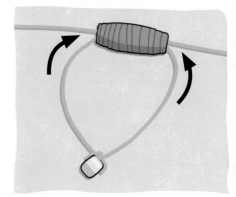

4 Thread both ends of the elastic through either side of a paper bead.

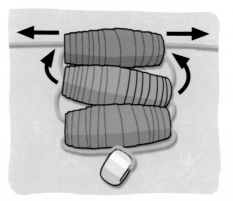

5 Continue threading the elastic through the remaining paper beads using the above technique.

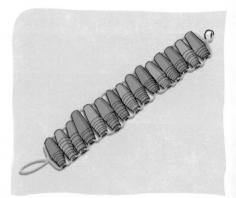

6 Tie a knot in one end of the elastic. Leave a small gap and tie another knot, then cut off excess. This creates a loop to go over the bead and hold your bracelet in plac

9 FELT ELEPHANTS

Holidays are a great time to go to the zoo. Why not make these cute elephants to remind you of your visit? Reuse the templates to make a whole herd!

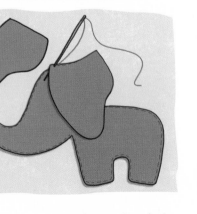

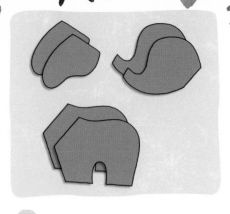

1 Use the templates for the large elephant from the back of this book. Cut out two of each piece from grey felt.

2 Sew the two head pieces together then sew the two body pieces together. Leave the straight neck area unsewn.

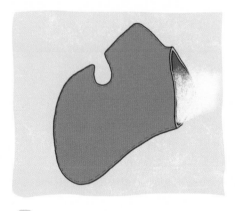

3 Fill both pieces with stuffing, using a pencil to push it into the corners. Make them nice and plump.

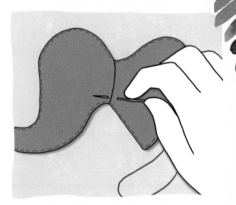

4 Sew the head to the body.

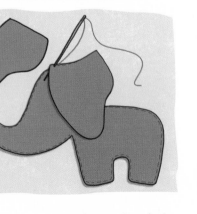

5 Put an ear either side of the head and sew in place.

6 Cut out two circles of white felt and draw on the eyes with a black pen.

7 Glue the eyes and a strip of grey felt for the tail to the body. Repeat the above with the smaller template for a baby elephant.

FISH KITE

Make this fun kite and see how high you can make it soar. Alternatively, you can just hang it up outside and watch it "swim" in the breeze!

1 Fold in and glue one long edge of an A3 piece of paper.

2 Turn the paper over. Cut out lots of circles of tissue paper. Starting from the unfolded end, glue the circles on for scales, overlapping slightly.

3 Leave a thick band of undecorated paper and make the last row of scales semicircles.

4 Cut some long streamers from tissue paper and glue to the back of the paper at the unfolded end.

5 Roll the paper into a tube and glue to hold.

6 Press out the eyes from the back of the book and glue to the fish's head.

7 Make 4 small holes around the fish's mouth and thread through a long piece of string. Tie to secure.

11 HOLIDAY BUNTING

Here's some quick and easy bunting for you to make, perfect for decorating any holiday or party occasion.

1 Draw around the templates onto a sponge and cut out. These are your stamps.

2 Pour some paint into a saucer or old jar lid and dip your stamp into the paint, then press the stamp onto a sheet of paper. Brown wrapping paper is great for printing on.

3 Stamp the palest colour first, repeating in patterns across your paper. Let this colour dry, then use a different stamp and darker colour to add another layer. Continue until you are happy with your design.

4 Cut out long triangles from your paper and tape to a length of string. Use to decorate your garden or have a garden-themed party indoors!

12 FINGER PUPPETS AND THEATRE

Holidays are a great time to put on a show. These cute finger puppets will help bring your stories to life - and they come with their very own theatre.

1 Press out the card pieces from the back of the book. Fold the stage along the dotted lines and stand up.

2 Glue the tabs of the puppets together so that they fit on your finger.

3 Give your characters names and let them take to the stage. Now all you need is a story: what do you think they might want to do?

13 MONSTER BOOKMARKS

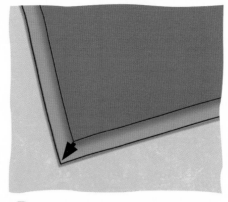

GRRR! Let these scary beasts keep guard over the page you're reading this holiday, and never lose your place again.

GRRRR

GRRRR

1 Glue two pieces of different coloured card together.

2 Use the template to trace and cut out the bookmark from this double-sided card.

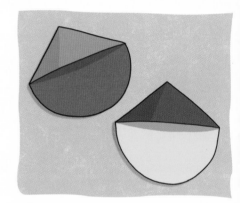

3 Fold the two pointed bits in to the middle. Glue the top piece to the one below.

4 The inside card looks like a tongue!

5 Add some of the press-out pieces for the monsters' features. Make sure you glue the teeth to the inside of the top piece.

6 Slip your little monster over the corner of your page.

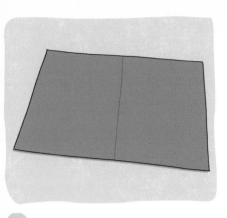

1 Fold a rectangle of coloured paper in half, then open up again.

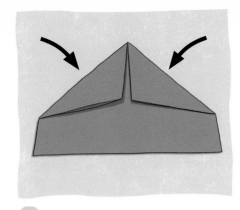

2 Fold the top two corners into the middle.

Make these paper boats to float on the pond, in a stream or maybe just in the bath!

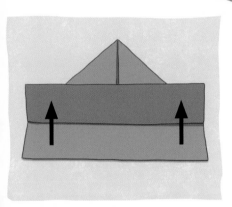

3 Fold up the bottom edge, turn over and repeat on the other side.

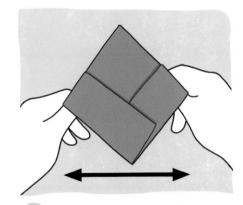

4 Pull the two flat edges out to make the corner ends fold flat as shown.

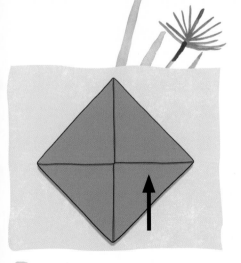

5 Fold the bottom up to the top, turn over and repeat with the other side to make a triangle.

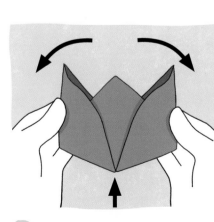

6 Pull the two flat sides out to make the triangular ends fold flat.

7 Use stencils at the back of the book for decoration. Pull out the sides and push up the middle as shown to create a boat.

15 SNAIL SANDWICHES

Fancy something different in your picnic? Why not try some snail sandwiches for a change!

1 Cut the crusts off three slices of bread.

2 Gently roll each slice with a rolling pin to make it thinner.

3 Add toppings to each slice, such as grated cheese and carrot, or a savoury spread of your choice.

4 Build up the three layers of bread with different toppings.

5 Carefully roll up your sandwich. Cut into sections.

6 Use cocktail sticks to add a tomato head and olive or cheese-chunk eyes.

7 Make a sweet version using a jam filling and a strawberry and grape head instead.

1 Use the template to cut out a bird body and wing from black card.

2 Cut lots of small squares of coloured card and glue to the black pieces, leaving small gaps between each coloured square.

3 Glue the wing to the body and make a round eye from white card. Cut a small triangle from black card and glue to the head for a beak.

4 Glue a clothes peg to the back of the bird.

5 Make up some more birds and peg to a twig or branch from the garden.

16 MOSAIC BIRDS

Tweet tweet! Create a flock of colourful mosaic birds and perch them on a branch.

17 SPINNING WINDMILLS

Give these bright and breezy windmills a blow and watch them spin around and around.

1 Glue two pieces of coloured paper together. Use the template at the back of this book to cut out the sail. Mark the middle point with a pencil.

2 Gently bend one of the cut corners into the middle and glue the end in place.

3 Leave the next corner flat. Bend the following corner and glue to the middle. Repeat with the remaining alternating corners.

4 Cut out a circle of card using the template and glue it into the middle of the sail.

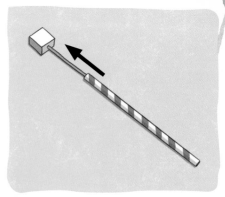

5 Carefully push a long wooden skewer into a rubber. Slide a paper straw over the skewer, flatten the top end and glue to hold.

6 Push a map or drawing pin through the middle of the sail and into the eraser. Do not push it in too tight or the sail will not spin. Now blow – and watch your windmill go!

1 Press out the card pieces and carefully fold inwards along the dotted lines.

2 Glue the small end tabs on the body to the folded-in legs.

FARM ANIMALS

Too wet for a walk in the country? Well, now you can bring the countryside into your home with these cute farmyard animals.

3 Glue the nose tab on the head to the folded-in sides.

4 Bend the long top tab back and glue the end to the body as shown.

5 Fold the chicken and glue the tops together.

6 Stand all your animals upright and gently bend their ears into position.

19 TROPICAL GARLAND

Aloha! Give your guests a warm, holiday welcome by placing this flower garland around their neck.

1 Turn a cake case inside out so the colour is on the inside.

2 Fold the case into quarters.

3 Fold it in half again then, cut off the edge as shown.

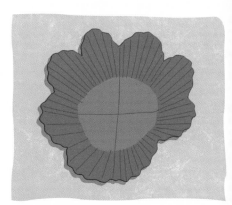

4 When you unfold the cake case, you should have a lovely flower shape. You will need about 60 flowers to make a nice thick garland.

5 Cut a long piece of string and use a needle to thread a flower. Cut straws into small 1cm pieces and thread between each flower.

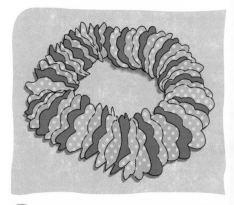

6 Continue threading flowers and pieces of straw until you have used all your flowers. Tie together the ends of the string to complete.

COLOURFUL SUNCATCHER

Create a glowing sun full of colour to brighten up your room, whatever the holiday season!

1 Press out the sun template at the back of this book. Place the small, pressed-out pieces onto tissue paper and cut around them, leaving a wide gluing edge.

2 Glue the tissue paper pieces to the back of the sun template.

3 Display the sun in a window, with the illustrated side facing inwards.

JELLY SANDCASTLES

These edible sandcastles are not only yummy – they're easy to make, too. Choose between a number of small sandcastles or a giant one with lots of smaller ones around it.

1 Fill some plastic cups with chopped fruit. Mix your jelly and pour over the fruit, then let it set in the fridge.

2 Press out the flags from the back of the book and glue to a cocktail stick.

3 Cut a slice of orange into a crab shape, push raisins into slits along the rind and give him some claws.

4 Take the jelly from the fridge and turn upside down to loosen from the cup. Serve with the crab. Put a flag in the top of the castle.

22 LOLLY STICK HARMONICAS

Keep everyone entertained this holiday with these fun and easy harmonicas. Make some for the rest of your family and see who can come up with the best tune!

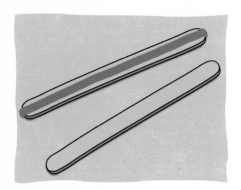

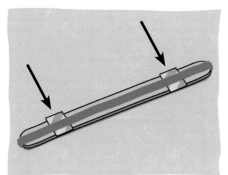

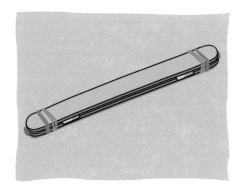

1 Take two lolly sticks. Around one of them, stretch a thick elastic band lengthways.

2 Cut two short pieces of paper straw or card and push them under the band near to each end of the lolly stick.

3 Place the other lolly stick on top of the first. Use small elastic bands to hold the ends together.

4 Place the long edge of the harmonica in your mouth and blow. See how loud you can go!

23 CRESS HEADS

Boiled eggs for breakfast? Don't throw away the shells – use them to make these fun egg folk with crazy cress hair.

1 Rinse out the shells. Soak a piece of folded tissue in water and place in each shell.

2 Sprinkle in some cress seeds.

3 Cut the bases from an egg box to stand your eggshells in.

4 Stick on some of the features from the back of the book to make funny characters.

5 Keep the tissue damp and the cress will grow. After a week you can give your cressheads a haircut. Yum!

1 Pre-heat oven to 180°C. In a bowl, mix 100g each of soft butter, caster sugar and self-raising flour. Beat in two eggs.

2 Place six cake cases into your tin. Spoon the mixture into each of the cases, filling them two-thirds of the way to the top.

3 Bake in the oven for 15 to 20 minutes (with adult supervision). The cakes are cooked when the top springs back if pushed gently.

4 Cool the cakes on a wire rack.

5 Mix 100g of icing sugar with 50g of soft butter and beat until you have smooth icing. Use a knife to spread the icing on the cakes.

6 Add sweets for ears. Cut short lengths of liquorice for the whiskers. Add chocolate drop eyes and a sweet nose.

24 MOUSE CAKES

Catch these quick and easy mouse-shaped cupcakes (if you can!). They look and taste really sweet!

SQUEAK

SQUEAK

25 FLYING PARROT

Every day's a holiday when you have a parrot as your friend. Watch him fly up and down, soaring high and low.

1 Press out all the card parts from the back of this book. Carefully fold the body sections inwards along the dotted lines.

2 Tape a coin to the inside of the flap indicated (the coin is to balance your parrot).

3 Cut a piece of string and tie to a bead, then thread through the hole on the bottom of the parrot and tie one end to secure.

4 Glue the tail tab to create a triangle.

5 Fold and glue the rest of the sections to the body.

6 Fold the head sections inwards.

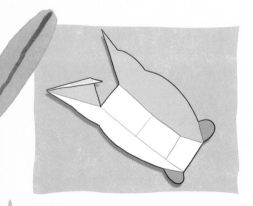

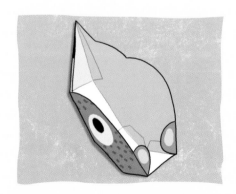

7 Glue the beak tab in place.

8 Continue gluing the rest of the sections to create the head. Fold the two semi-circle tabs inwards and add a dot of glue to each.

9 Slide the head over the body and gently press to stick the glue.

10 Cut a piece of string and thread through the hole in the wing. Tape both ends to the inside of the wing.

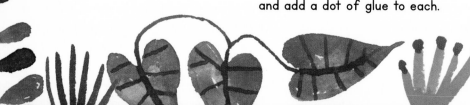

11 Tape two coins to the inside near the shaped end. These act as a weight to balance the wings. You may need to adjust these in steps 17-18.

12 Fold the wing along the dotted lines and glue the long sides, leaving the feathered end open to add more coins if necessary. Repeat with the other wing.

13 Slide the wing into the slit and lift to lock tabs into notch. Repeat with the other wing.

14 Press out the tail feathers and fold along the dotted lines to make a fan shape.

15 Glue the tips of the two long outside feathers together to secure.

16 Glue the long side of the tail feathers to either side of the body. Gently fan the feathers out.

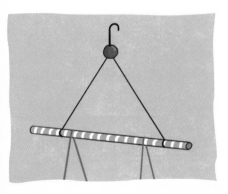

17 Slide the wing strings over each end of a paper straw. Attach a hook and string and hang the straw. To balance the wings, add more coins (as step 11).

18 When the wings are level, seal their ends and tape the wing strings to the straw. Gently pull the bead, moving the parrot's body downwards to see it flap its wings.

YOU WILL NEED

General equipment: Scissors, paper glue, white glue, pencil, coloured paper, coloured card, string, straws, adhesive tape, needle and thread. Project components are either pressed out of the card sheets or traced from the templates and stencils.

The lists below indicate what materials and equipment are needed for each project in addition to the general items (left). Items in bold are those supplied on the tear-out sheets at the back of the book.

1 PEBBLE BUG HOOPLA
Card sheet, pebbles, paint and paintbrush, black felt

2 TWIGGY PICTURE FRAME
Twigs, pieces of card, picture

3 WOVEN FLOWERS
Templates, wool, straws or safety pins

4 POMPOM BUNNIES
Card sheet, wool, felt

5 BUTTERFLY STRAWS
Card sheet and templates, paper cups

6 SEASIDE MOBILE
Card sheet

7 JUMPING FROG GAME
Card sheet, templates

8 BEAD BRACELET
Templates, thin elastic, plastic bead

9 FELT ELEPHANTS
Templates, coloured felt, stuffing

10 FISH KITE
Card sheet, A3 piece of paper, tissue paper, string

11 HOLIDAY BUNTING
Templates, paint, sponges, brown wrapping paper (or similar)

12 FINGER PUPPETS AND THEATRE
Card sheet

13 MONSTER BOOKMARKS
Card sheet

14. PAPER BOATS
Card sheet

15 SNAIL SANDWICHES
Bread, knife, rolling pin, cocktail sticks, sweet or savoury fillings and garnishes

16 MOSAIC BIRDS
Template, clothes peg, twig or branch

17 SPINNING WINDMILLS
Templates, rubber, wooden skewer, map or drawing pin

18 FARM ANIMALS
Card sheet

19 TROPICAL GARLAND
Cake cases, string

20 COLOURFUL SUNCATCHER
Card sheet, tissue paper

21 JELLY SANDCASTLES
Card sheet, plastic cups, chopped fruit, jelly, cocktail stick, orange, raisins

22 LOLLY STICK HARMONICAS
Lolly sticks, elastic bands (large and small)

23 CRESS HEADS
Card sheet, eggshells, tissue, cress seeds

24 MOUSE CAKES
100g butter, 100g caster sugar, 100g self-raising flour, 2 eggs (for cakes), 100g icing sugar, 50g butter (for icing), sweets for decorating, mixing bowl and spoon, cake cases and tin, wire rack, knife

25 FLYING PARROT
Card sheets, coins, bead, hook

Copyright © Quarto Children's Books, 2017
Published in the UK by QED Publishing
Part of the Quarto Group, The Old Brewery,
6 Blundell Street, London, N7 9BH
All rights reserved
ISBN 978-1-78493-783-6
Printed in Shaoguan, China.
1 2 3 4 5 19 18 17 16 15

Author Fiona Hayes
Illustrators Carolyn Gavin, Jessica Secheret
Design Duck Egg Blue
Editor Matthew Morgan
Creative Director Jonathan Gilbert
Publisher Zeta Jones

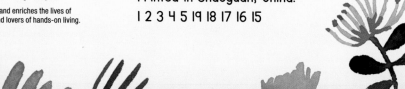

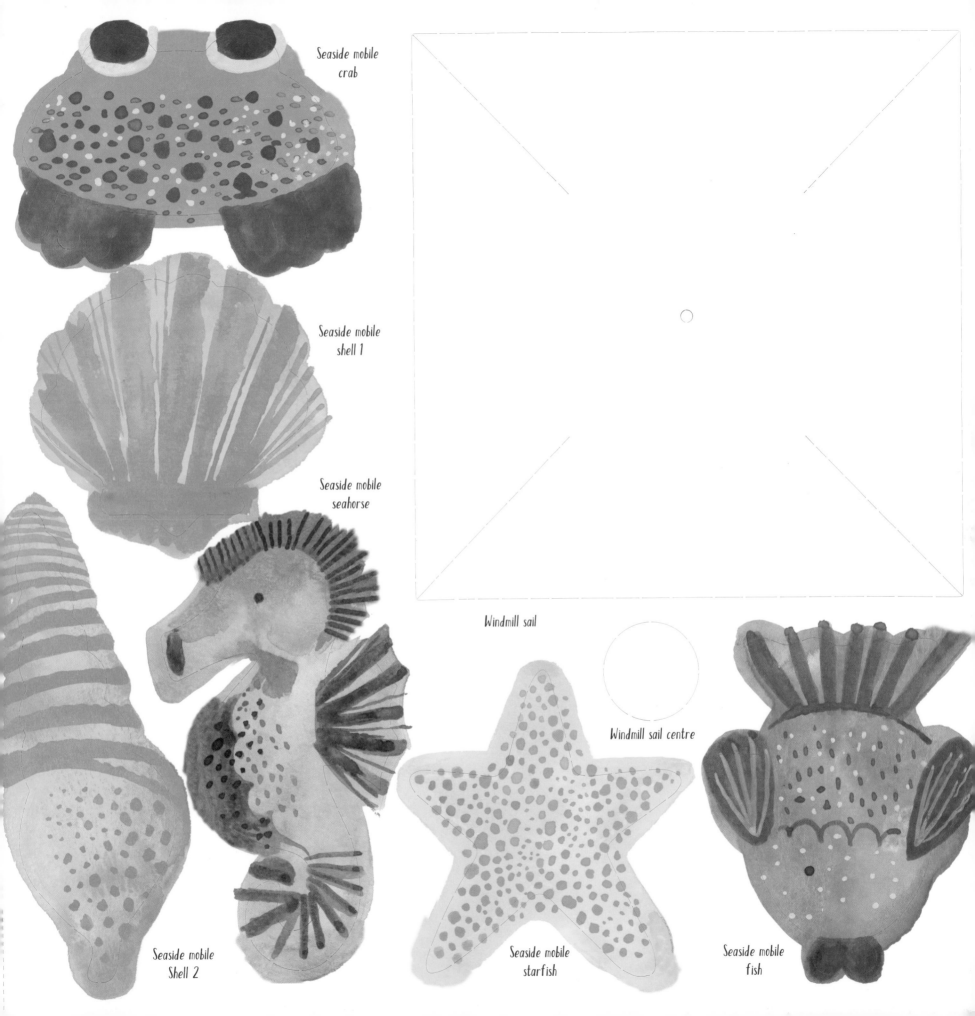

Seaside mobile
crab

Seaside mobile
shell 1

Seaside mobile
seahorse

Windmill sail

Windmill sail centre

Seaside mobile
Shell 2

Seaside mobile
starfish

Seaside mobile
fish

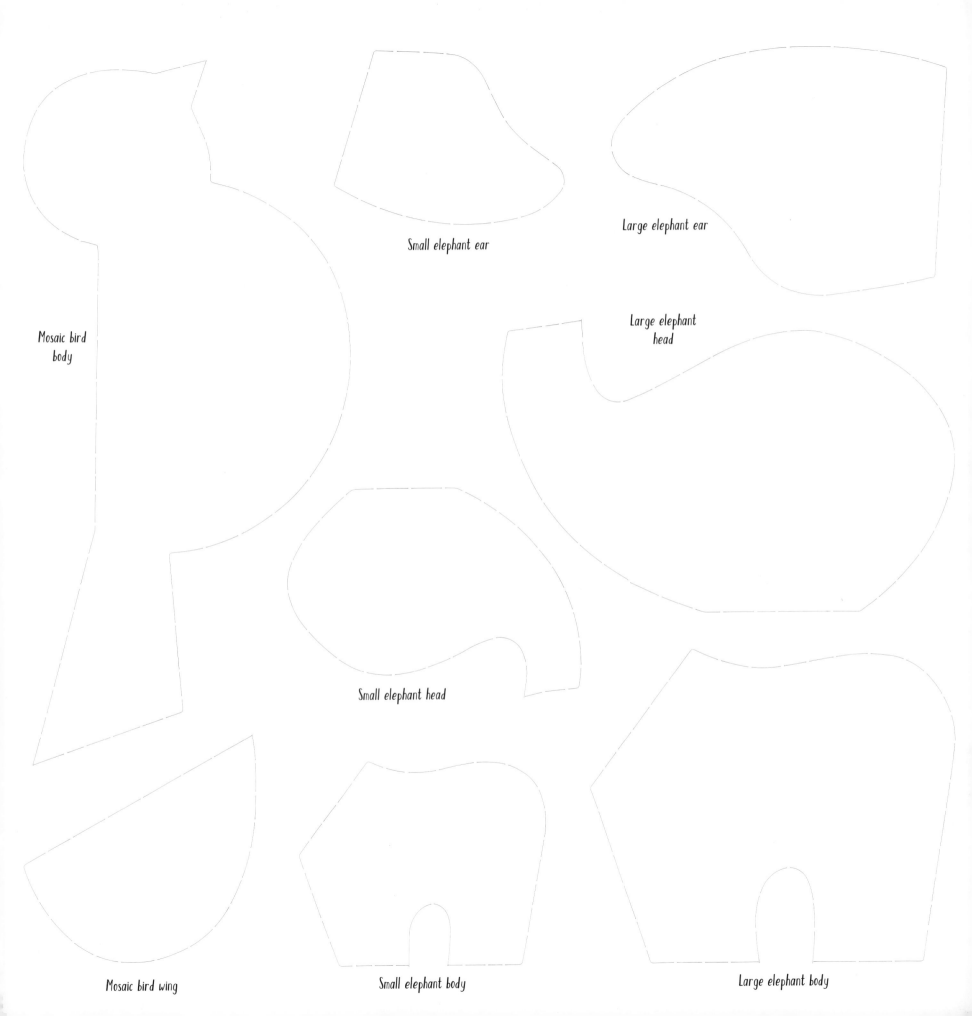

Small elephant ear

Large elephant ear

Large elephant head

Mosaic bird body

Small elephant head

Large elephant body

Mosaic bird wing

Small elephant body

Large elephant body

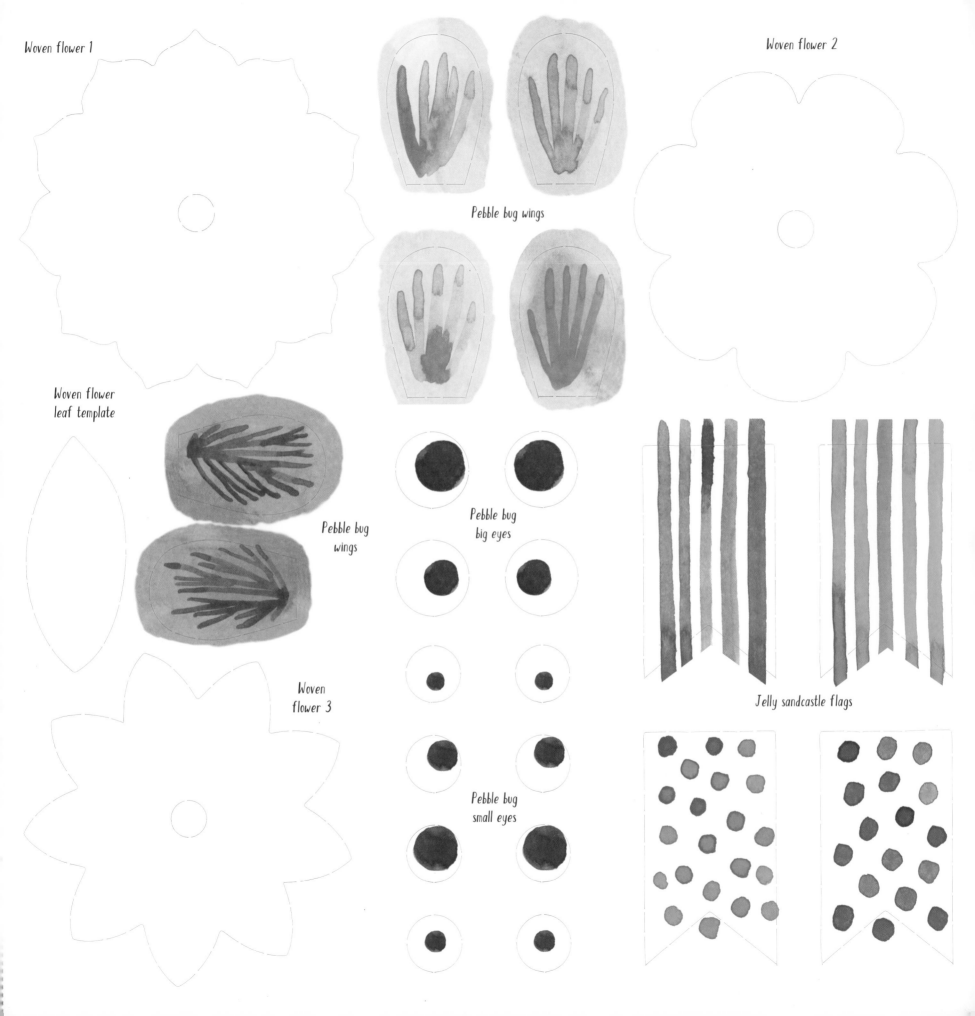

Woven flower 1

Woven flower 2

Pebble bug wings

Woven flower
leaf template

Pebble bug
wings

Pebble bug
big eyes

Jelly sandcastle flags

Woven
flower 3

Pebble bug
small eyes

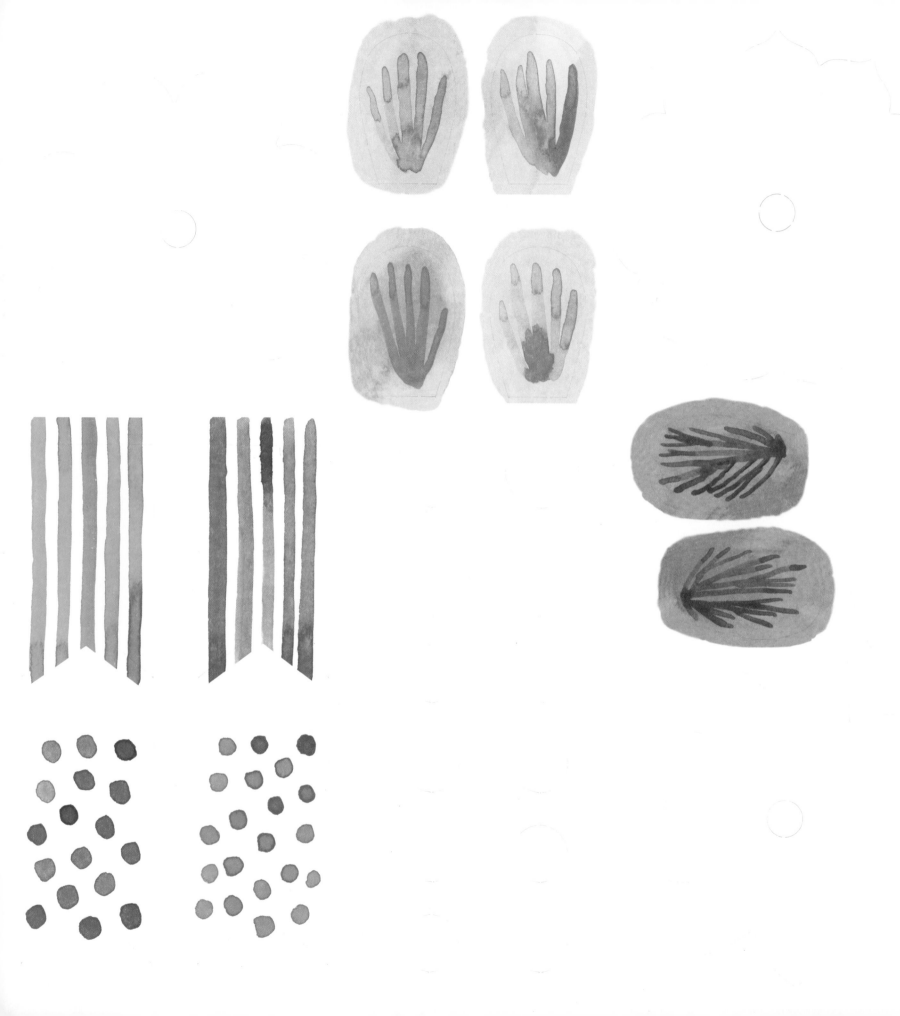

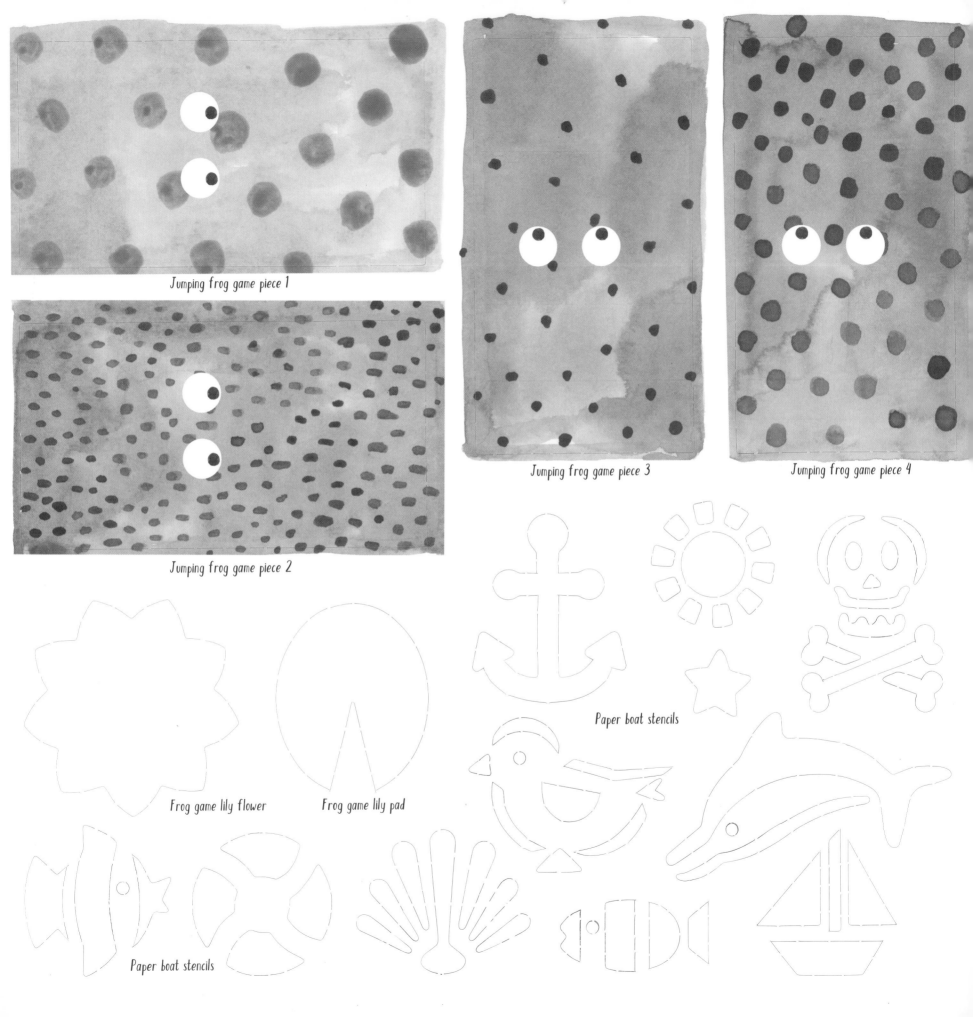

Jumping frog game piece 1

Jumping frog game piece 2

Jumping frog game piece 3

Jumping frog game piece 4

Frog game lily flower

Frog game lily pad

Paper boat stencils

Paper boat stencils

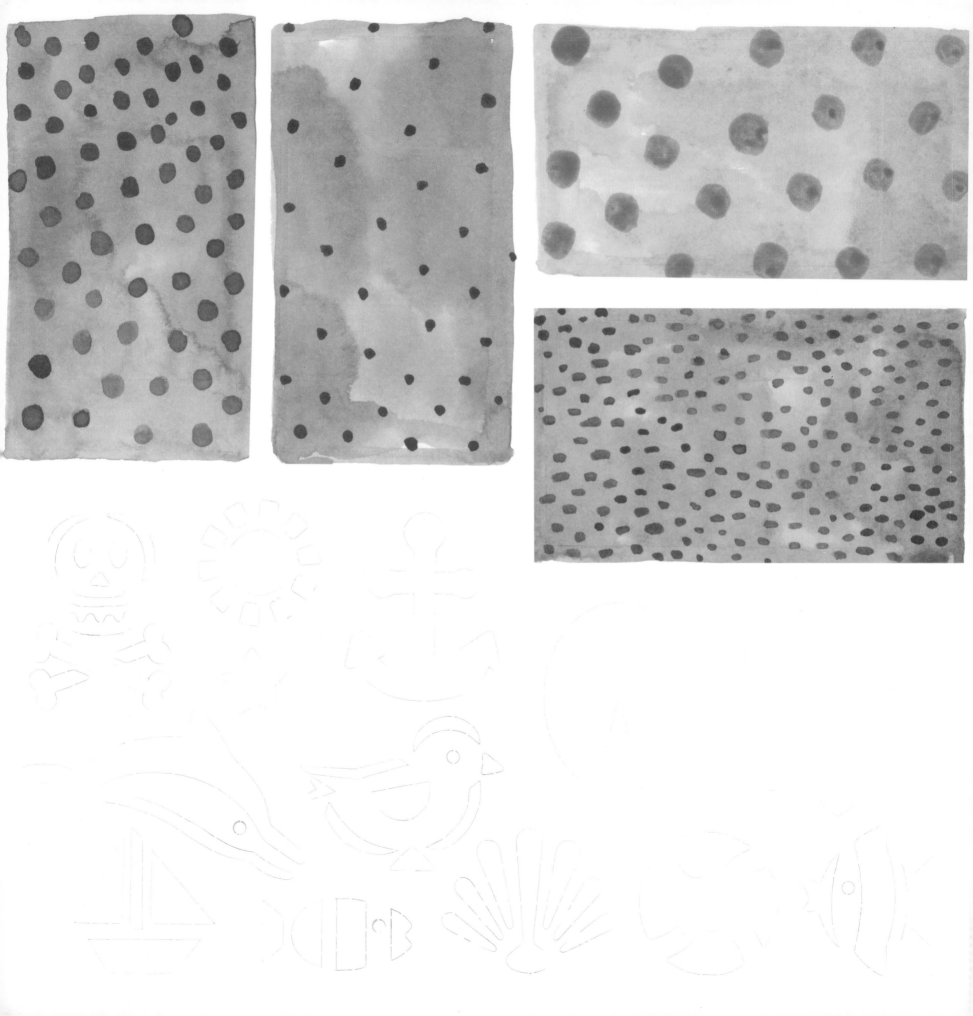

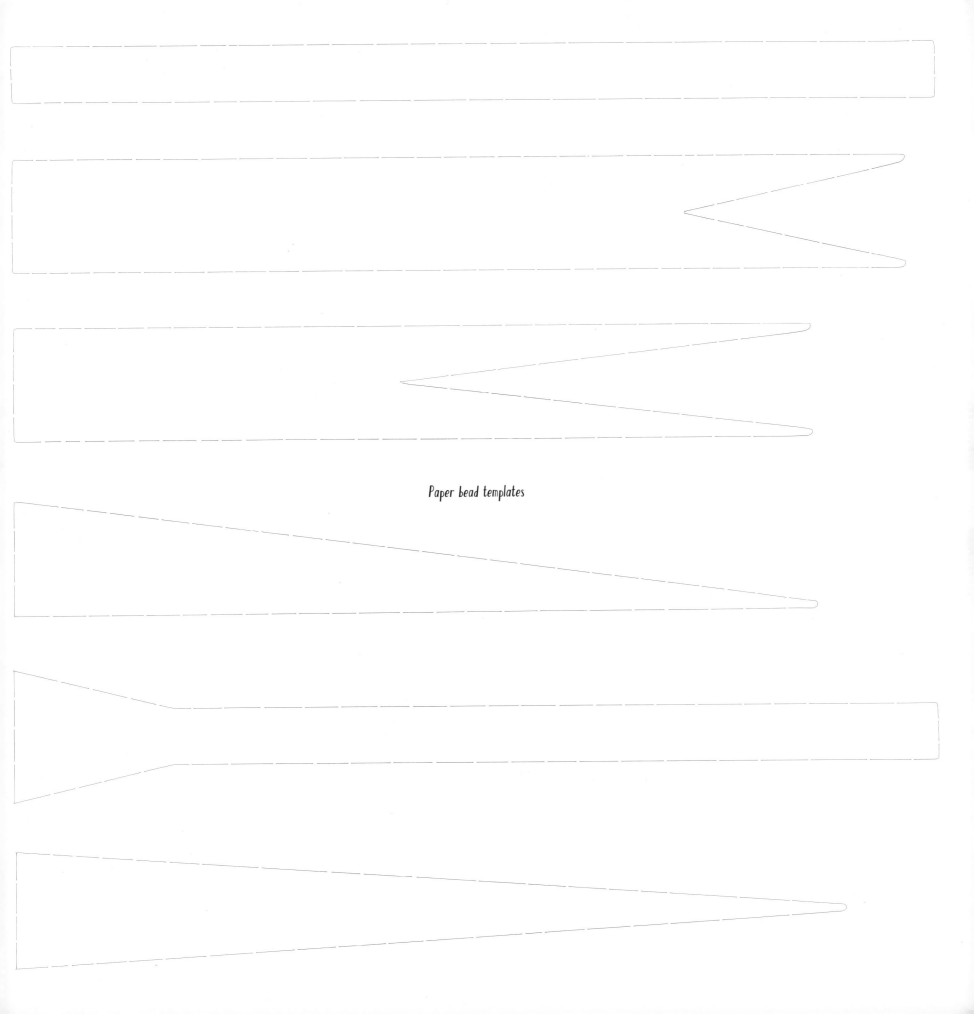

Paper bead templates

Theatre

Cat finger puppet

Dog finger puppet

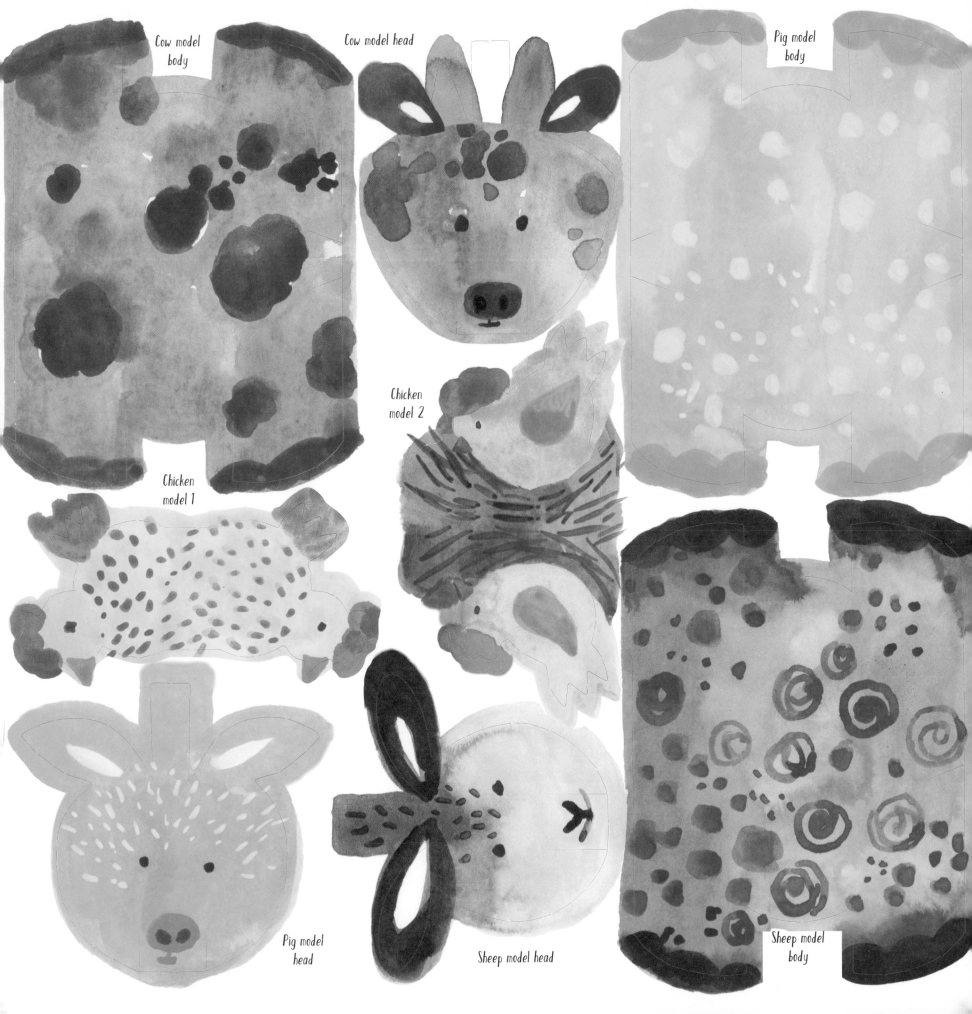

Cow model body

Cow model head

Pig model body

Chicken model 2

Chicken model 1

Pig model head

Sheep model head

Sheep model body

Holiday bunting
big heart

Holiday bunting
flower

Suncatcher

Holiday bunting
star

Holiday bunting
small heart

Butterfly straw 1

Butterfly straw 2

Butterfly straw 3

Butterfly straw 4

Butterfly straw 5

Monster bookmark fangs

Monster bookmark eyes

Monster bookmark template

Monster bookmark horns

Monster bookmark teeth

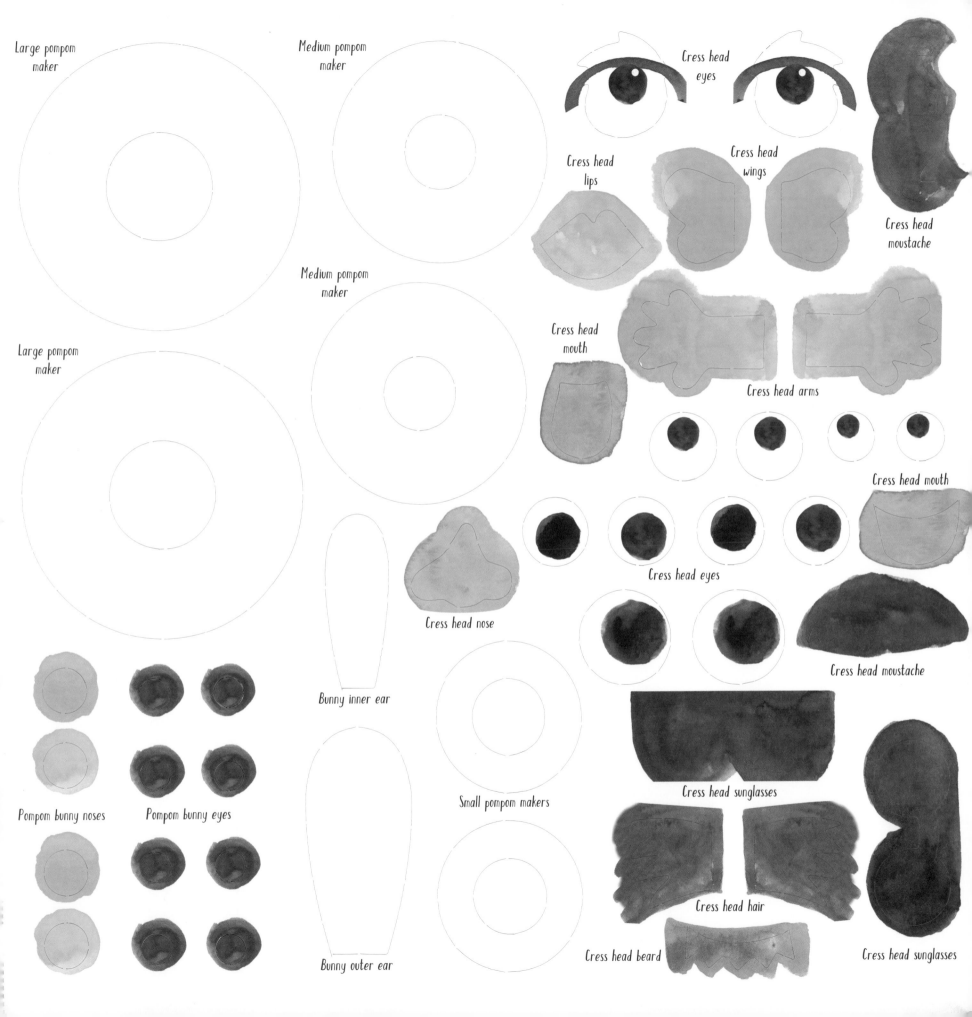

Large pompom maker

Medium pompom maker

Cress head eyes

Cress head wings

Cress head lips

Cress head moustache

Medium pompom maker

Cress head mouth

Cress head arms

Large pompom maker

Cress head mouth

Cress head eyes

Cress head nose

Cress head moustache

Bunny inner ear

Cress head sunglasses

Pompom bunny noses

Pompom bunny eyes

Small pompom makers

Cress head hair

Bunny outer ear

Cress head beard

Cress head sunglasses

Flying parrot head

Flying parrot
wing 1

Flying parrot
wing 2

Flying parrot
body

Fish kite eyes

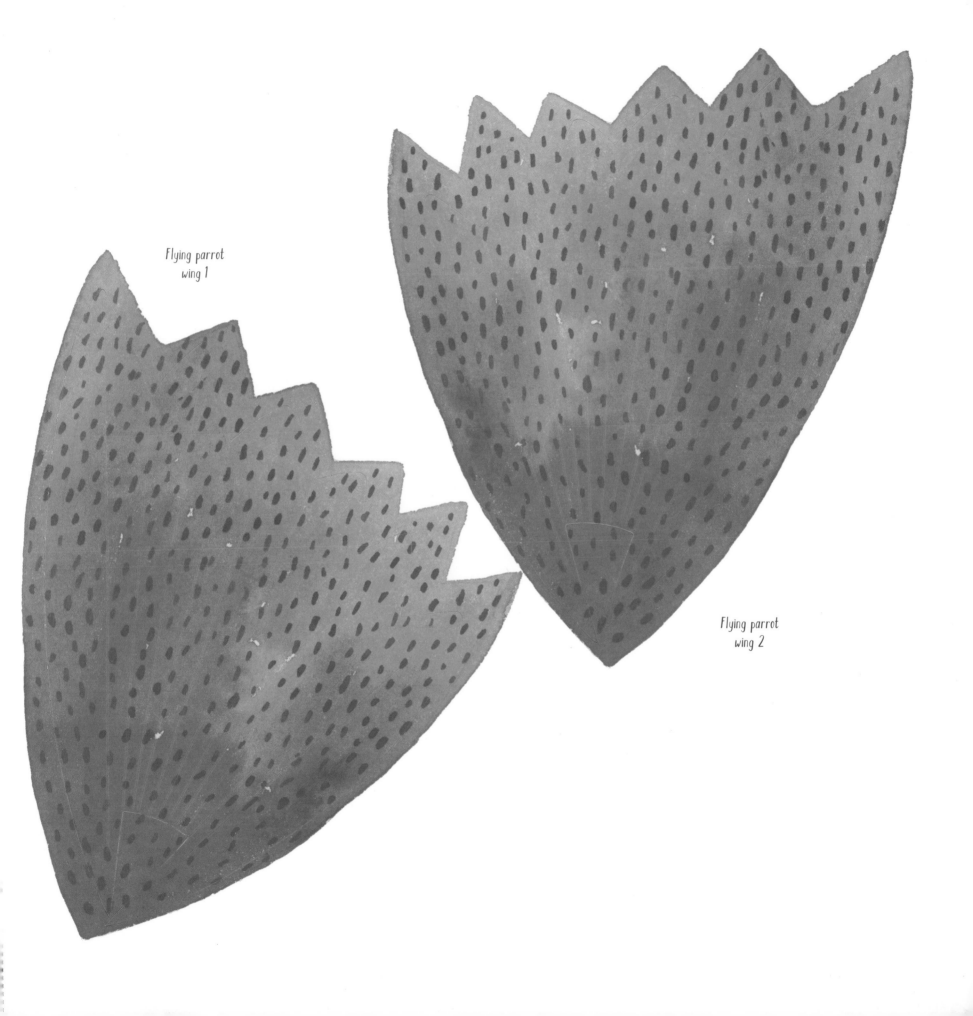

Flying parrot
wing 1

Flying parrot
wing 2

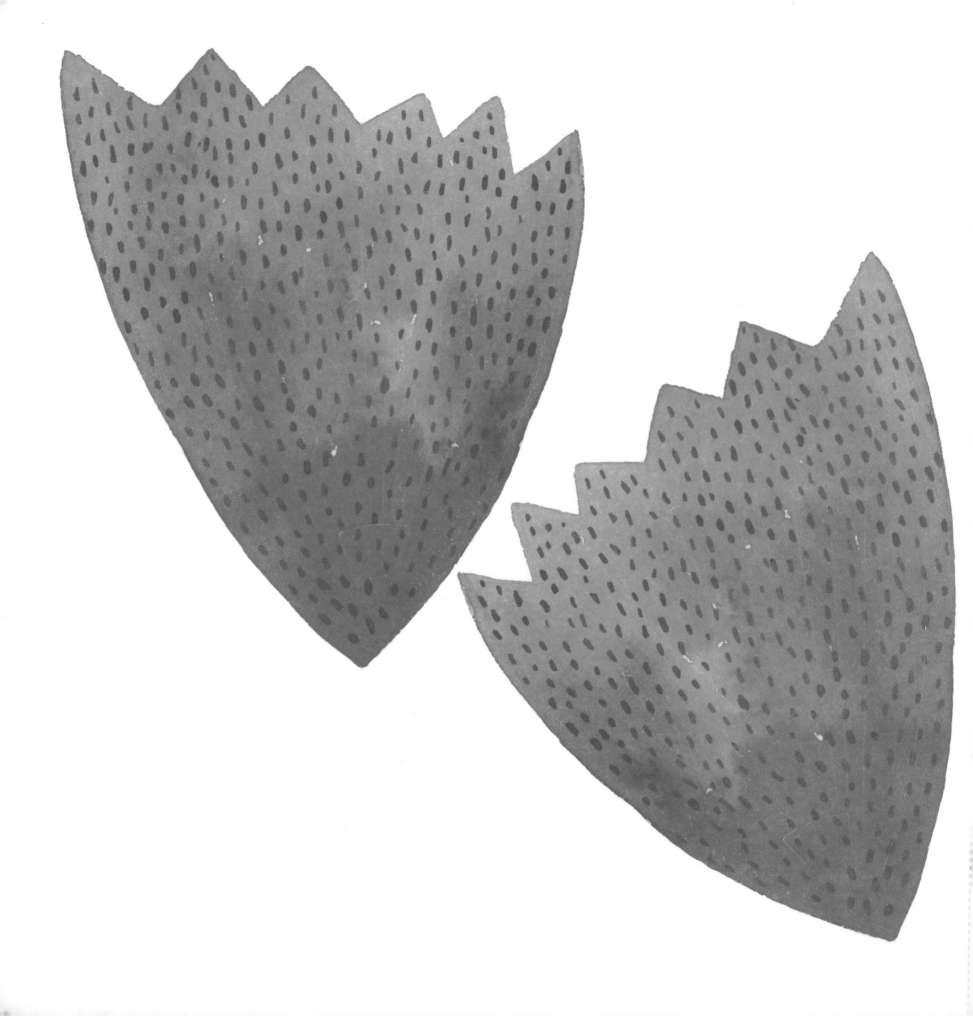